Weapons of War

From Axes to War Hammers:
Weapons from the Age of Hand-to-Hand Fighting

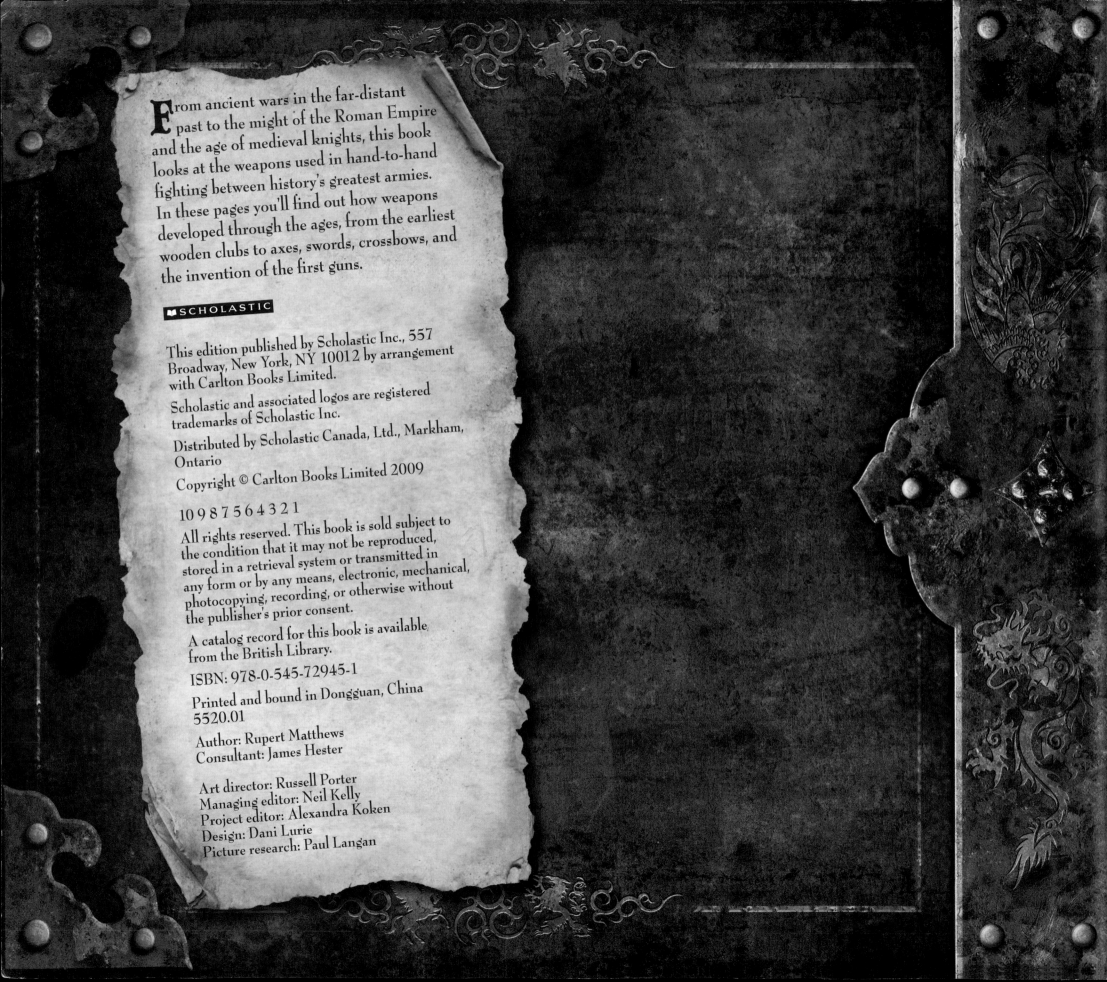

From ancient wars in the far-distant past to the might of the Roman Empire and the age of medieval knights, this book looks at the weapons used in hand-to-hand fighting between history's greatest armies. In these pages you'll find out how weapons developed through the ages, from the earliest wooden clubs to axes, swords, crossbows, and the invention of the first guns.

SCHOLASTIC

This edition published by Scholastic Inc., 557 Broadway, New York, NY 10012 by arrangement with Carlton Books Limited.

Scholastic and associated logos are registered trademarks of Scholastic Inc.

Distributed by Scholastic Canada, Ltd., Markham, Ontario

Copyright © Carlton Books Limited 2009

10 9 8 7 5 6 4 3 2 1

A catalog record for this book is available from the British Library.

ISBN: 978-0-545-72945-1

Printed and bound in Dongguan, China
5520.01

Author: Rupert Matthews
Consultant: James Hester

Art director: Russell Porter
Managing editor: Neil Kelly
Project editor: Alexandra Koken
Design: Dani Lurie
Picture research: Paul Langan

WARRIORS

AGE OF CONQUERORS

Weapons of War

Tales of Ancient & Medieval Warfare by

Rupert Matthews

SCHOLASTIC

From Axes to War Hammers:
Weapons from the Age of Hand-to-Hand Combat

Stone to Metal

Human beings aren't very strong. We don't have sharp claws, big teeth, or pointed horns, but we do have hands for making things and intelligent brains for coming up with new ideas. Thousands of years ago, our ancestors began to invent weapons to help them hunt for animals and fight against rival human beings.

Ancient Evidence

Prehistoric humans (above) used simple clubs as weapons. Over time, new weapons were invented. The 4,000-year-old cave painting shown here (above right) features a man carrying a bow.

Stone and Wood

Many prehistoric weapons were made of stone. Spearheads and arrowheads (left) were made of flint or obsidian (a kind of volcanic glass), because they were easy to shape and very sharp. Sharpened wooden sticks were also used as spears and arrows.

In some places people continued to use these ancient weapons—in the rainforests of South America, native tribesmen still use them today! But other people were discovering metal, and soon they were making their weapons out of this stronger material.

Flint Arrowheads

The First Weapons

Everything we know about early weapons comes from finds by archaeologists (people who study the remains of humans from the past) and the pictures that prehistoric people—humans who lived before written records began—left on cave walls. The first edged, or sharp, weapons were made about 1.9 million years ago. These were large pebbles that had one side chipped away into a sharp edge. Archaeologists call them "choppers." As people evolved, so did their weapons. Choppers became hand axes, which were gradually replaced by weapons such as axes, spears, bows, and slings.

The First Americans *This flint spearhead (above) was made by a group of prehistoric people called the Clovis. They lived in the Americas about 13,000 years ago. The flints they made have a distinctive, pointed shape. Archaeologists believe that the Clovis hunted large animals called mammoths that have now died out, or are extinct, because their flints have been found with mammoth bones.*

David and Goliath
In the Bible, the sling (left) was used by David to slay the giant, Goliath. Slings are simple but deadly. A stone from an ancient Egyptian sling can travel farther than an arrow shot from a bow of the same time period. As well as stones, slings could hold bullets made of lead or clay. Ancient Greek lead bullets were sometimes engraved with pictures such as thunderbolts, or defiant phrases such as "Take that!"

Egyptian Sling, 700 BC

Boomerang

Early Metal Weapons

About 5,500 years ago people started making weapons out of copper. By adding tin to copper they developed bronze. This is a much stronger metal, and it allowed a blade or point to stay sharp for longer. New types of weapons, such as swords and daggers, were forged out of this stronger metal, as well as better versions of existing weapons, such as spears or arrows.

About 3,500 years ago, people learned how to make iron, and then steel. These metals were even stronger than bronze. Soon all weapons were made from iron or steel.

Changing the Course of History

Over time people have developed more effective and increasingly lethal weapons. There have been lots of different styles and types produced by different tribes, cultures, and armies throughout history and around the world. This book tells the stories of some of these weapons, how they were made and used, and how they changed the world forever.

Deadly Blow
In South America, tribesmen still hunt with blowpipes. The darts are often poisoned to paralyze prey.

Smart Stick
Australian Aboriginal people are famous for making a special weapon called the boomerang (above). This wooden throwing stick is shaped so that it can fly a long distance. Some fly in a straight line, while others return to the user. Boomerangs are not just found in Australia—examples have been found all over the world. The oldest boomerang ever found is made of mammoth tusk and was discovered in a cave in Poland. It is thought to be about 30,000 years old!

Spears

Depending on its length, a spear can be held in one or both hands and is used to thrust at an enemy. It was a popular weapon for thousands of years because it was cheap and easy to make, and brutally effective on the battlefield. Some armies developed special fighting tactics that turned units of soldiers with spears into killing machines.

Early Spears

The earliest spears were simple wooden poles with one sharpened end, but by about 100,000 years ago people had improved them by attaching sharp flints to one end. When metalworking was developed, bronze spearheads were among the first weapons to be made. The Hittites (above left), who lived in what is now modern Turkey, were some of the first people to discover iron. They used it from about 1500 BC to make the spearheads of the long spears they carried when riding into battle in their war chariots.

Greek Hoplites

In around 700 BC, a new type of soldier called a hoplite was fighting in the Greek army. These fierce warriors fought with a short spear called a dory. It was around 9 ft. (2.7 m) long and was held in one hand. For protection they wore a helmet and carried a large, round shield. Hoplites fought in a formation called a phalanx, which in Greek means "finger." Standing shoulder to shoulder in a solid mass up to eight men deep, they locked their shields to form a wall of defense. With the first few rows of soldiers pointing their spears forward, the phalanx marched steadily toward the enemy. The men at the back used their shields to keep pushing the front rows toward their foes.

Greek Soldiers, ca. 400 BC

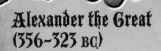

Alexander the Great (356–323 BC)

Alexander, king of Macedon, led an army that conquered many countries. He created an empire that stretched from India to Greece, and is considered to be one of the greatest leaders in history. One of the keys to Alexander's success was the sarissa (see below) and the strictly disciplined, tight phalanxes that his troops formed to use it.

Macedonian Phalanx, ca. 330 BC

Macedonian Sarissas

Around 350 BC, the Macedonian Greeks developed the sarissa. Measuring around 20 ft. (6 m), it was much longer than any other weapon of the time and needed to be held with two hands. The Macedonians also fought in tight phalanxes, as you can see from the picture above. No enemy was able to withstand this deadly wall of spikes. As the Macedonians advanced, the enemy was pushed aside or impaled on the lethal sarissas.

Celtic Terror

In battle, the Celts had a fearsome reputation. Instead of relying on strict discipline and formation, they charged at a run, screaming as they went, and clashing with the enemy in a frenzied and animal-like attack. Some Celtic spearmen, or Gaesatae, even fought naked, protected only by a special necklace called a torc. Imagine how terrifying that sight would have been!

Fact file
Celtic Spear
Weight: 2–4 lbs. (1–1.8 kg)
Length: 6–8 ft. (1.8–2.4 m)
In Use: 5th–1st century BC
Origin: Northern Europe

Prized Possessions

In early Western Europe, the spear was one of the main weapons used by the Celts. If you look carefully at the spearhead below, you will see a delicate design engraved into the metal. The time and effort that went into making and decorating this weapon show us how important spears were to the Celts.

Saxon Spear, ca. AD 450

Saxon Spears

The Saxons used iron-tipped spears with ash shafts (poles), like the one above. Ash was the perfect wood to use because it was light but also strong, and less likely to break.

European Warfare

Around the year AD 900 in Europe, some mounted soldiers began to carry a type of spear called a lance. It was longer than a normal spear and was held straight out, supported under the arm, while the soldier charged the enemy at a gallop. The aim was to hit the opponent with the end of the lance. Men who used lances were usually part of a military elite that became known as knights. These men and the lances they carried were an important part of European warfare for over 400 years.

After about AD 450, the footsoldiers' spear was replaced by a longer weapon called a pike. At 13–16 ft. (4–5 m) long, it was hard to wield and had to be held in two hands. Pikemen attacked in formations that were six or more rows deep, holding their long pikes forward horizontally. The lines of spikes protected men with muskets (early guns), who fired through the pikemen at the enemy.

By the AD 1700s, pikes and spears had fallen out of use on the battlefields of Europe.

Sucking Spear *Zulu warriors in Africa carried short spears called iklwas for fighting at close quarters.*

English Civil War Pikemen

Javelins

The javelin is a light spear that is designed to be thrown. It was probably one of the first missiles, or flying weapons, to be invented. The simplest javelin was a wooden shaft, or pole, with one sharpened end. More sophisticated javelins had sharpened flints tied to the end of the shafts with leather or a form of twine.

Aztec Using a Throwing Stick

SPEAR-THROWERS

The spear-thrower was invented about 30,000 years ago. It is a long piece of wood, bone, or antler with a handle at one end and a notch at the other. The spear is fitted into the notch and then thrown. The throwing stick acts as an extension of the thrower's arm, giving more power to the throw (above). This throwing stick, or atlatl (right), was used by the Aztecs, who lived in what is now Mexico. The Aztecs were fierce warriors who captured prisoners in battle to use as human sacrifices to their gods.

Aztec Throwing Stick

KANGAROO HUNT *This painting (left) shows Australian Aboriginal people hunting some very strange-looking kangaroos with their javelins!*

Simple Javelins

Ancient wooden javelins have not survived to the present day because they have rotted away over time, but sharpened flint tips have been found. From studying these flints, experts believe that prehistoric people were using javelins about 50,000 years ago.

The simplest javelins were soon adapted to make them more accurate and give them a longer throwing range. Tapering, or trimming, the shaft to make the widest part closer to the point made the weapon heavier at the front. This made it more stable in flight and easier to aim.

Over time the javelin evolved into a very accurate and important weapon of war for armies all over the world.

Fact file
Roman Pilum
Weight: 2 lbs. (1 kg)
Length: 7 ft. (2.1 m)
Range: 82–164 ft. (25–50 m)
In Use: 150 BC–AD 300
Origin: Roman Empire

ROMAN ATTACK!
As well as killing and wounding, the pilum was useful for slowing down enemies and making them easier to attack. On the order of their commander, the massed Roman soldiers hurled these weapons at the enemy lines. If a pilum hit a shield, it often stuck in it, making the shield too heavy and awkward to use. Forced to lower or drop their shields, any unprotected soldiers were at the mercy of the advancing Romans.

Thessalians *These Thessalian soldiers from northern Greece were skilled at throwing javelins from horseback.*

Greek Javeliniers

By about 700 BC, some Greek armies had special units of javelin throwers, known as javeliniers. At the start of a battle they raced forward, throwing their javelins as hard as they could at the lines of enemy soldiers facing them. Javeliniers did not need to wear much armor because they usually retreated before the main fighting began between the heavily armored soldiers.

Some tribes specialized in javelin fighting. The Thessalians, Thracians, and Agrianians, who lived north of Greece, and the Mysians, from what is now Turkey, were famous and fearless javelin fighters. They were so good that they were often hired by other countries to help fight wars.

The Roman Pilum

Every soldier in the Roman army was taught to use a special sort of javelin called a *pilum* (left). It had a short wooden shaft with a long, thin metal "shank" that connected the spike to the shaft. The shank was held on by wooden pegs. When the pilum made contact with a target, the pegs snapped and the shaft fell off. This made it impossible for the enemy to pick it up and throw it back.

Soldiers threw their pilums before the main charge, then they drew their swords and ran at the enemy for the main battle.

After the Romans, other armies continued to use javelins. But as the bow became more powerful and accurate, it slowly replaced the javelin in many parts of the world. From the AD 1000s, javelins were hardly used at all in Europe and Asia.

Roman Battle Tactics *The formation above repelled enemy cavalry (mounted soldiers). A wall of shields and pilums, angled up toward the horses, protected the throwers. Once the enemy was close, the weapons were released.*

Roman Pilum

Julius Caesar (100–44 BC)

From 59–51 BC, Caesar fought a war to conquer Gaul (modern France and Belgium) for the Roman Empire. All Roman soldiers were trained in the javelin. One of Caesar's most successful battle tactics was to use this skill in the early stages of battle to disrupt and scatter enemy formations.

Saddle Up *Jereed was a popular sport in the Ottoman Empire in Turkey. Points were scored by throwing blunt javelins at other horsemen.*

Short Swords

The short sword might be less impressive to look at than the long sword, but it was just as deadly. In single combat or open battles, it was not as powerful as the longer slashers. But in close-combat battles, where soldiers were packed tightly together in a terrifying crush of men and weapons, the short sword was perfect for stabbing and thrusting into the enemy.

Daggers and Swords

About 3000 BC, when people began making things out of metal, weapon makers started to forge daggers out of bronze. These early daggers had wooden handles with a short metal blade about 8 in. (20 cm) long. The blade was attached to the hilt, or handle, with leather straps or bronze rivets (a bolt or pin). By 1500 BC, these daggers had been lengthened and transformed into short swords.

Soldiers, especially spearmen, often carried short swords or daggers to use if their main weapon got broken or lost on the battlefield. In Thrace (an area of the southern Balkans north of Greece), the men who specialized in throwing javelins also carried a short, curved dagger called a *sica*. These javeliniers usually retreated once they had thrown their weapons, but sometimes they got caught up in the main fighting. Their sicas gave them a chance to protect themselves from the onslaught if they hadn't been able to retreat in time.

Leonidas (520–480 BC)

Leonidas was king of the Spartan people of ancient Greece. When Persia attacked Greece in 480 BC, Leonidas led a force of just 1,400 men—300 of whom were Spartans—against the mighty 80,000-strong Persian army. Surrounded at the narrow pass of Thermopylae, his men threw away their broken spears and fought on with their short swords. All of Leonidas's men were killed, but their bravery is now legendary and is featured in the movie 300.

European Bronze Dagger, ca. 1000 BC

Roman Dagger and Scabbard

This is what a Roman dagger and scabbard would have looked like about 2,000 years ago (right).

Roman Gladius

Around 300 BC, in Spain, people started to use a special type of short sword. It had a wide blade that tapered to a long point and was sharpened along both sides, right down to the tip. This weapon could be savagely thrust around, under, or over the enemy's shield, and was especially good in close combat. The Romans adopted this Spanish weapon and it soon became the standard sword used by Roman soldiers. They called it a *gladius* (below), which is Latin for "sword."

Roman Gladius

The Gladius: Ideal for Roman Warfare

A Longer Blade

After the decline of the Roman Empire in around the second century AD, fighting in close ranks was replaced by more open tactics, with more space to move. Short swords weren't good for this style of fighting because it involved slashing and swinging, so soldiers began to use longer swords.

By AD 1300, medieval knights were carrying swords that could stab and slash. These were about 39 in. (1 m) long and had a wide, flat blade with a sharpened end.

Civilian Weapons

Around AD 1500 the *cinquedea* (below) became popular in Italy. *Cinquedea* means "five fingers," and refers to the wide width of the blade. It was carried by ordinary people for protection against robbers and bandits, and some even used it in heated brawls.

Meanwhile, the gentlemen of Europe preferred to carry a more sophisticated weapon: the rapier. It had a thin, steel blade about 43 inches (1.1 m) long and the hilt had a metal hand guard for protection. It was the mark of a gentleman to carry such a sword and the rapier became a common dueling weapon.

By around AD 1660, guns were becoming popular and short swords began to be replaced by bayonets: a type of dagger that soldiers attached to the ends of their rifles.

Persians Fighting in Close Combat, AD 627

Italian Cinquedea, ca. AD 1500

Long Swords

S wishing through the air in the heat of a fierce battle, the long sword was a terrifying and powerful weapon that could inflict hideous wounds. On the open battlefield, when men found themselves fighting for their lives in single combat, it reigned supreme.

The Rise and Fall of the Long Sword

The oldest known long swords were made of bronze in Europe around 1000 BC. They are known as "leaf" swords (below), because of the shape of the blade. The blade and hilt were cast in one piece, which reduced the risk of the blade snapping off in combat.

Around 600 BC, the Persians developed a long sword with a curved blade that was sharpened on one side. Centuries later, they were still using short curved swords (left) called cutlasses. The Greeks also had a curved sword called a *kopis*. It was used mainly by the cavalry (mounted soldiers), who slashed the razor-sharp blades down from their horses at attacking infantry, or foot soldiers.

About AD 350, the Romans started using a long sword called the *spatha*. This was probably because their battle tactic of fighting in close formation had changed to a more open style. Now they could swing and slash at their enemy, rather than just stab.

By AD 1100, in Europe, the sword had become a secondary weapon. Poor people could not afford them. A rich nobleman now rode into battle with a long lance as his main weapon, and only used a sword if his lance broke.

Persian or Arabic Cutlass

Celtic Leaf Sword, ca. 1000 BC

A Horrible Death

This man was killed by a slashing blow from a long sword across the face. His skull was dug up by archaeologists at the site of one of the bloodiest battles in English history. About 28,000 men died in one day at The Battle of Towton, England, in AD 1461.

VIKINGS! *The Vikings of Scandinavia were masters of the long sword (left). These costly weapons were often richly decorated and specially made for each warrior.*

William Wallace (ca. AD 1274–1305)

William Wallace led Scotland in a war of independence against England. A terrifying sight on the battlefield, he is thought to have fought with a giant claymore sword. Wallace was captured by the English in AD 1305, found guilty of treason, and executed. This picture shows Mel Gibson as Wallace in the movie Braveheart.

Scottish Claymore Sword, ca. AD 1300

After AD 1350, the armor used by knights became so heavy and strong that swords were almost useless against it. This meant that knights began to use other weapons. At the same time, swords became cheaper to make, so an ordinary soldier could at last afford to carry a sword of his own. By AD 1400, most infantrymen were equipped with a sword that was about 32 in. (80 cm) long. It had a sharp point for stabbing and a double-edged blade for slashing.

The Great Swords

In the AD 1400s, some highly trained men serving in Germany began to use a very long and heavy sword called a hand-and-a-half-sword (left). A similar weapon was used in the Highlands of Scotland and parts of Ireland. This great sword was the *claidheamh mhor* (above), which means "great sword" in Gaelic. Today, it is most often called the claymore. Warriors needed to be very strong and skilled to use great weapons like these.

Cavalry Swords

Guns became the main weapon on the battlefield from the AD 1500s. Foot soldiers fought with muskets and pikes instead of swords, but it was hard to load a gun on horseback. Cavalrymen continued to use their long cavalry swords.

German Hand-and-a-Half Sword

JAPANESE SWORD *The samurai were a fierce warrior-class of soldiers that lived in medieval Japan. They used a katana (above): a type of long, curved sword with a razor-sharp blade. The sword was carried with the blade upwards so it could slash an opponent as it was being drawn. Katanas were made of a special Japanese steel. Each sword could take weeks, or even months, to make.*

Two Hands

This medieval knight's weapon shows how long some swords were. This one is almost as tall as a man and needed two hands to wield it.

Maces

The mace was a vicious weapon that was used all over Europe from the AD 900s, the middle years of the medieval period (ca. AD 476–1500). It was fairly short, so warriors could swing it at each other in hand-to-hand combat. It inflicted severe wounds, and a single blow to the head could kill a man outright. Even if he survived, a soldier hit with a mace could often no longer fight and was left in agony.

German Mace

Fact File
German Mace
Weight: 4–9 lbs. (1.8–4 kg)
Length: 24–35 in. (60–90 cm)
In Use: AD 900–1650
Origin: Germany

Wooden Clubs

The mace was based on the wooden club. The earliest clubs were simply wooden sticks, but from 9,000 years ago people started tying stones to the end to make them more effective.

After bronze was invented, people stopped using wood and stone maces because the stones shattered on impact with metal. By about 500 BC, maces and clubs weren't used at all, but around the year AD 900 the mace became popular again. The reason for this was mail armor.

Mail Armor

Mail is a type of flexible armor that is made up of metal rings, linked to form a mesh. Many soldiers wore it for protection against slashing weapons like long swords. Only heavy arms, such as the two-handed ax, could injure a man wearing mail, but these were large and difficult to use. A lighter weapon was needed, and the answer was the metal mace.

A 14th-Century European Battle

Fijian Warrior

Before European sailors arrived, there was no metal on the island of Fiji, so weapons were made of wood. The most deadly was the pineapple club (above). It was shaped like a mace and had a spike that penetrated the skull and killed instantly.

Dreadful Injuries

The mace inflicted terrible injuries, but if treated quickly they were rarely fatal. A crushed skull and damaged brain meant almost certain death, but more usual injuries were broken arms or legs. Simple breaks could be strapped to a wooden frame and often mended well, but a heavy blow could shatter a bone into tiny fragments. If the soldier survived this, he was often left with a horribly deformed limb.

The Metal Mace

The metal mace (left) had a metal head and a wooden handle. The round head weighed about 4.5 lbs. (2 kg) and the handle was around 24 in. (60 cm) long. This was short enough to avoid getting caught up in close combat, but long enough to get a good, hard swing at an opponent.

Maces were not designed to pierce mail armor. But because mail was flexible, when the mace smashed into the wearer, the force of the blow was brutal. Even a mild blow inflicted severe bruising, and heavier blows broke bones.

European Metal Mace, ca. AD 1550

Flanged Mace

Not surprisingly, men began wearing padded shirts underneath their mail for protection. By around AD 1150, the flanged mace had been invented to combat this. Both of the large maces shown here (left and far left) are flanged maces. If you look closely, you can see the thin metal rims on the head. These made the point of impact smaller and more intense, which made padded shirts far less effective for protection.

Gradually, maces became less popular on the battlefield. Yet because they were cheap and easy to make, peasants continued to carry them in rebellions and riots right up to the early sixteenth century.

The Brutal Norman Bishop *One of the most famous men to use a mace was Odo, bishop of Bayeux, at the Battle of Hastings in AD 1066. As a bishop, Odo was not really supposed to shed the blood of his fellow Christians, so he used a mace to crush their bones instead. He probably commissioned the famous Bayeux Tapestry, which shows him raising his mace at another soldier (above).*

Military Flail *The long, wooden handle of this evil-looking weapon had one or more spiked, metal balls attached to it by chains. The balls were swung around and around before being smashed into the opponent. The flail delivered a far more powerful blow than a standard mace, but it was a difficult weapon to use in close combat.*

War Hammer *During the late medieval period, the mace was replaced by the war hammer. This weapon (below and left) looked like the kind of hammer used for driving nails into wood, but its purpose was to penetrate armor.*

Axes

Axes have been used for thousands of years, and are one of man's earliest weapons. It takes strength to swing an ax, but when it meets its target the sharp blade can slice through flesh and bones, and even light armor.

Ancient Axes

Some of the earliest prehistoric tools were stone ax heads that were made to be held in the hand. These are called hand axes. About 70,000 years ago people began to fix these ax heads onto wooden handles, so that they could be swung at a target with more force. The first metal axes were made from copper, and by 1500 BC bronze axes were being made in lots of styles.

Most ancient Egyptian soldiers carried an ax about 16 in. (40 cm) long that was slung from the belt and used as a secondary weapon. The royal guards of the Hittites, who ruled in what is now Turkey, had two types of ax. The larger one was 4 ft. (1.2 m) long and had two blades. The Assyrians preferred a small ax with three sharp spikes pointing back behind the blade, possibly to puncture armor.

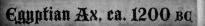

Egyptian Ax, ca. 1200 BC

Two-handed Danish Ax

Tomahawks

Originally, these axes were made of stone. They were used by Native Americans as tools and as weapons in close combat and for throwing. Metal tomahawk heads were introduced by European settlers to trade with the Native Americans. They were based on British Royal Navy boarding axes.

Tribal Warfare

After about 400 BC, axes became less popular. Battles became struggles between densely packed and tightly controlled units of men and there was no room to swing an ax with any real effect.

As the Roman Empire disappeared, so, too, did its controlled battle tactics, and axes became popular again. The Franks, a Germanic tribe that conquered Gaul and renamed it *Frankreich* (much of modern France), used an ax called the francisca. It was a throwing ax about 16 in. (40 cm) long that could split shields in half and punch through armor.

The Vikings

In Scandinavia, by about AD 800, a new type of war ax was being used. This was the type of ax favored by the Vikings. The Danish ax, as it became known, had a blade around 12 in. (30 cm) across. The blade was slightly curved and usually angled downward so that it could be brought down into its victim.

Two hands were needed to use this ferocious weapon. It was swung around and around the body, high in the air, before being slammed into its target. It took great strength and years of practice to wield this ax properly, so it was only used by full-time soldiers. The Danish ax was used until about AD 1200.

DECORATED AX *This small, beautifully engraved ax was found in the tomb of a Viking nobleman in Mammen, Denmark, and dates from around AD 971. It may only have been used in special ceremonies, but axes like it were also employed in hand-to-hand combat and could be thrown with ease.*

The Mammen Ax, ca. AD 971

Erik Bloodax (d. AD 954)

The Viking leader Erik Bloodax got his name from his favorite weapon and his savage temper. He inherited the throne of Norway from his father, Harald Fairhair, in AD 930. Erik was deposed by one of his brothers and fled to England, where he ruled the Viking-controlled city of York. He led many raids on Scotland and died in AD 954 in a battle against the English.

Medieval Europe

By AD 1100 knights in Europe were riding into war. The two-handed Danish ax was impossible to swing on horseback so it became less popular. Some mounted men still used smaller axes with shafts of about 31 in. (80 cm) and heads with a thin cutting edge. These were designed to punch through armor. Foot soldiers carried axes that were slightly longer. These weapons also had a wider cutting edge for smashing into other, less protected, foot soldiers.

After AD 1400, axes were rarely carried by professional soldiers. Only poor men, who were called up for short-term army service, still took the wood-cutting axes that they used on their farms into battle.

Scotland remained the only place in Europe where war axes were still used. Scottish infantry soldiers carried a short ax with a curved blade until the middle of the 16th century.

OFF WITH HER HEAD! *The ax was often used to execute people. The prisoners would lay their necks on a wooden block and the "headsman" would chop their head off.*

Pole arms

Fact file
English Poleax
Weight: 18–22 lbs.
(8–10 kg)
Length: 6–10 ft.
(1.8–3 m)
In use: AD 1450–1600
Origin: England

During the late medieval period, pole arms were in general use among ordinary infantry, or foot soldiers. These multipurpose weapons could slash, chop, hook, and stab, while keeping the enemy at a distance.

Plate Armor

By the AD 1400s, knights were wearing heavy armor called plate armor. It was made up of sheets of metal that were shaped to fit the knight's body. Plate armor was better than mail armor because it deflected sharp points and protected the wearer from heavy blows. The usual weapons carried by infantry soldiers, such as maces, were useless against it and a new weapon needed to be invented.

Pole arms developed from the heavy spears that peasants took into battle. These spears were useful against horses and foot soldiers, but not against fully armored knights. Adaptations were made to improve them, such as the addition of sharp ax heads, spikes, and hooks.

James IV · King of Scots

BATTLE OF FLODDEN In AD 1513, Scotland invaded England. The rival armies met at Flodden, the Scots armed with pikes and the English with bills (see opposite page). The Scots were defeated and the body of their king, James IV (above), was found with five bill wounds.

Death by Poleax

Poleaxes (above) could thrust like a spear and chop like an ax. The hook on the back of the ax head was used to pull an enemy over, or off his horse. Once he was lying on the ground in heavy armor, he was almost helpless.

Swiss Halberd ca. AD 1600

English Poleax, AD 1460

European pole arms came in many shapes and sizes. This Swiss halberd is an example of a beautifully crafted weapon.

The English Bill In the AD 1450s the English developed a special pole weapon called the bill (below). It combined the ax and spike into one curved blade.

"Langets"

Pole arms had one serious weakness. The heavy metal head was fitted to a wooden pole that could easily be chopped into by an enemy sword or another pole arm, leaving the soldier holding nothing more than a wooden pole! To stop this from happening, pole weapons were fitted with metal strips, known as "langets," that ran down the handle and protected the wooden staff.

Bodyguards

By the AD 1550s, instead of poleaxes, infantry began to use either a long, spear-like pike or an early type of gun called a musket. But bodyguards continued to use pole arms for some time. They preferred to use them because they had a longer reach than a sword and did not need to be reloaded like a gun. As late as AD 1640, the men of the English Royal Bodyguard were equipped with pole arms. Even today, members of the Swiss Guard, which protects the pope at the Vatican, in Italy, are still armed with a type of pole weapon.

Stay Sharp! Beefeaters at the Tower of London in England still carry pole arms called partizans (right). Although they are ceremonial, they are still razor-sharp!

"Good Morning"

Known as the goedendag ("good morning"), this pole weapon was used to great effect by the Flemish infantry against French knights at the Battle of the Golden Spurs in AD 1302. It was made up of a thick, wooden pole with a metal spike on top. Its name is thought to have come from the sarcastic taunts of the Flemish troops to the French on the morning of the battle.

The Naginata

This Japanese pole arm (right) was developed in around AD 750. It was originally used for fighting mounted warriors, but by AD 1250 it was mostly being used by women to defend their homes against bandits. The naginata allowed them to keep a man at a distance, where his greater height would not be an advantage.

The Face of Battle

This skull belongs to a soldier who was dug up by archaeologists at the site of the Battle of Towton, England, which happened in AD 1461. He was killed when a poleax swung into the left side of his face. Medieval battlefields were often very crowded. Some men died from suffocation—crushed by the force of their own men pushing them from behind—or by being knocked to the ground and trampled.

Dueling Weapons

Fact file
Spanish Rapier
Weight: 4.5 lbs.
(2 kg)
Length: 39 in.
(1 m)
In use:
AD 1550–1700
Origin: Spain

A duel is a fight between two people, carried out under strict conditions to make sure that both combatants, or fighters, have an equal chance of winning. In the past, these fights were controlled, but they were brutal and violent. Often, the two combatants fought to the death.

Gladiator Games

The earliest known duels were between gladiators (shown left) in the arenas of the Roman Empire. The first gladiators were slaves who fought to the death at the funeral of their master, using whatever weapons were available. Later, these brutal fights became organized, popular public shows. By 100 BC, gladiators had become highly trained professionals who fought using a standard range of weapons and equipment.

Most gladiators were men, although some were women. Many were unfortunate slaves and others were tough criminals who were sentenced to serve as gladiators for a period of time. Only a few were volunteers, attracted by the fame and money.

During the fight a referee made sure none of the rules were broken. If a gladiator was defeated, he could ask for mercy by raising the first finger of his left hand. The man paying for the show then decided if the loser should live or die. If the loser had fought well he might live; if not, the winner would kill him.

Who Will You Support?

There were several types of gladiators. Thracians fought with short, curved swords and small, square shields; Murmillos used the standard swords and shields of the Roman army; Hoplomachos had a spear and a small, round shield; and the Provocators used slashing swords and hexagonal (six-sided) shields. Most had helmets and armor on their arms and legs, except the Retiarius. He fought without armor or a helmet and used a trident (a three-pronged spear) and net as weapons.

MEDIEVAL SWORDSMANSHIP

Fighting manuals such as this one were written in Germany around AD 1290. They contained illustrations with instructions on how to fight.

Medieval Tournaments

In medieval Europe, knights competed in tournaments that gave them a chance to practice their fighting skills in preparation for war. Some tournaments involved chaotic mock battles between groups of knights. A combat between two knights armed with similar weapons was called a joust. By about AD 1350, jousts had become more formalized and began with knights charging one another with lances while riding horses. In the AD 1500s, jousting with lances was a popular sport among noblemen, even though they rarely used the skill in battle anymore. The sport died out in the AD 1600s.

Trial by Combat

In Europe, dueling probably developed from trial by combat. This was common among people from prehistoric Germanic tribes. A person accused of a crime could challenge the accuser to a fight. If the accused won, he was declared innocent. If he lost—which usually meant being killed—he was considered to be guilty. Dueling became less common after AD 1600, but it was not banned in Britain until as late as AD 1820.

Sword Duel, AD 1617

Henri II (AD 1519–1559)

King Henri of France liked to fight. He launched many wars against different countries and loved to show his skill with weapons at tournaments. He was killed as a result of a jousting accident. A sharp piece of wood from a splintered lance entered his helmet slit. Eleven days later, he died from an infection.

LANCES *The lances used in jousts were similar to those used in warfare. The only difference was that they were often made of soft wood that would shatter on contact. This made the fight more spectacular, and it was easier to decide if a hit had been made. A joust might continue with swords if the lances did not produce a winner.*

AN OLYMPIC SPORT *In the sixteenth century, it became common for men to settle arguments by fighting a duel. They usually fought with rapiers. These swords were lighter and more flexible than the swords used in warfare. Special schools were even set up to teach men how to fight in duels. These skills have survived in the sport of fencing, which is still included in the Olympics.*

Bows

Until guns became widely used in the AD 1500s, the bow was one of the most effective ways of launching missile weapons. Developed in prehistoric times, it was used for hunting and warfare for thousands of years.

An Assyrian Archer, ca. 645 BC

Early Bows and Arrows

Early bows were made from a single piece of wood with a bowstring of animal sinew or plant fibers. These bows shot arrows up to 328 ft. (100 m). The first arrowheads were made of carefully shaped stone. Examples have been found that are almost 50,000 years old. By 500 BC, people were making arrowheads out of bronze.

Ancient Egyptians from the 800s BC used simple bows about 63 in. (1.6 m) long. From the 600s BC, Assyrian archers (above) used bows that were similar to those employed by the Roman army. They shot light wooden arrows fitted with bronze arrowheads. These caused nasty wounds, but could not pierce armor or shields —armies relied on slingers and javeliniers to achieve this.

English Longbow

Fact file
English Longbow

Weight: 5.5 lbs. (2.5 kg)
Length: 71 in. (1.8 m)
Range: 984 feet (300 m)
In use: ca. AD 800–1600
Origin: England and Wales

Quiver
Archers kept their arrows in a quiver. This sixteenth-century samurai warrior (left) has five arrows in a quiver on his back. The arrows have feather fletches to help them fly.

Composite Bows

Sometime before 800 BC, the people living on the plains of central Asia invented a new type of bow. There were few trees growing on the plains, so long, single pieces of wood were in short supply. To get around this problem they glued smaller pieces of wood, horn, and sinew together to make a "composite" bow with a distinctive double-curved shape. Although it was only around 39 in. (1 m) long, it was as powerful as larger wooden bows and far easier to shoot from a horse.

Arrows with Feather Fletching

Mongol Empire *Mongolian archers were deadly with the composite bow, especially from horseback. Led by their infamous and cruel leader Genghis Khan, this skill helped them conquer a huge empire.*

The Deadly Longbow

The longbow (left) was being used in Western Europe by about AD 500. It was almost 79 in. (2 m) long and made from a single piece of yew or fir wood. It shot arrows 984 ft. (300 m) with enough force to pierce armor.

The longbow was used all over Britain, but the English specialized in it. To make sure it was widely practiced, King Edward I of England (AD 1239–1307) even banned all sports on Sundays except archery. This way he knew there were plenty of good archers available should he ever need them.

Look Out: Arrow Storm!

In the AD 1330s, the English developed a new battle tactic: the "arrow storm" (below). Previously, archers had mixed with ordinary soldiers and shot at specific targets. The English decided to put their archers in a group and trained them to shoot clouds of arrows into the sky towards the enemy. Medieval armies were often closely packed together, so the arrows usually found a target.

The longbow was most famously used by the English against the French at the Battle of Crécy (AD 1346). Here, the firing rate of one to two bolts per minute from the crossbows on the French side was no match for the English longbow firing rate of one shot every five seconds!

Arrow Loops *Medieval castles were built with special cross-shaped windows called arrow loops (left). Archers could fire safely at attackers without the risk of being hit themselves.*

English Arrow Storm

Arrowheads

The longbow shot specialized arrows.

(1) *The barbs on flesh-piercing broadheads made them hard to pull out without ripping a wound open.*

(2) *Short points, or bodkins, could punch through plate armor.*

(3) *Even horses weren't safe. This "horse galler" was designed to bring a horse down and dismount its rider.*

(4) *Long, narrow bodkins could slide in between the gaps in mail armor.*

(5) *Fire arrows shot balls of flaming cloth. Fire caused havoc in castles and among troops.*

1
2
3
4
5

Robin Hood (Twelfth Century)

One of the most famous longbowmen was Robin Hood, an outlaw who is said to have lived in Sherwood Forest, England. According to legend, he and his gang robbed from the rich and gave to the poor, but many of the stories we hear about him are folktales. Tales of Robin Hood are just as popular today, and many movies have been made about him. This picture shows Kevin Costner in Robin Hood: Prince of Thieves.

Crossbows

The crossbow was used for centuries in Europe and Asia. It was accurate, had a long range, and shot with devastating power. Crossbows were easy to operate, and ordinary soldiers made good use of them. In medieval battles, the air was filled with the sickening thud of crossbow bolts finding their targets.

European Crossbow, ca. AD 1600

Drawing a Crossbow

A crossbow can be made of wood, metal, or a mixture of horn and sinew. The bow part is mounted sideways on a wooden stock (a long handle). This has a trigger mechanism and a groove along which the bolt (a short arrow) is loaded. When the bow is drawn, the bowstring is pulled back to a hook that holds it tight. The bolt is then slotted into the groove and the weapon is aimed. When the trigger is pulled, the hook releases the bowstring, which shoots the bolt forward. The bowstring is pulled back to exactly the same place every time, so it is easy to judge how far the bolts will fly.

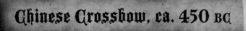

Chinese Crossbow, ca. 450 BC

Early Crossbows

The crossbow was probably invented in about 1000 BC, by tribes that lived in what is now Mongolia. By 450 BC, it was being used by the mighty armies of ancient China. The earliest Chinese record referring to the weapon describes its effectiveness in an ambush at the Battle of Maling in 341 BC.

From 350 BC, the ancient Greeks were employing a small crossbow called a *gastraphetes,* or "belly weapon." To aim the weapon, the user braced the curved centerpiece of the butt end against his chest or belly. The Romans also used small, bolt-firing crossbows, but it was not until medieval times that the weapon became widely used in Europe.

Wind It Up *Around AD 1370, the powerful windlass crossbow (right) was invented. It had a pulley system that was operated by a pair of handles. When these were turned, the bowstring was pulled tightly back into position. This made the windlass crossbow easy to reload and about four times as powerful as a longbow.*

William Tell (ca. AD 1285–1354)

According to legend, William Tell was a farmer living in the canton (member state) of Uri, Switzerland, at the time when Duke Albert II of Austria was imposing his rule on the area. Tell refused to obey the new laws and taxes introduced by the king, so as a punishment, he was ordered to shoot an apple from his son's head using his crossbow. Luckily, Tell had good aim and hit the apple, not his son! Tell went on to lead an uprising that threw the Austrians out of Switzerland.

Crossbowmen in Battle

In medieval Europe, crossbowmen from Genoa, in Italy, were famed for their shooting abilities. These mercenaries (soldiers who fought for whoever paid them) caused heavy losses. In AD 1248, Emperor Frederick II, ruler of the Holy Roman Empire, suffered defeat at the Battle of Parma, Italy. The skills of the Genoans played a major part in the battle, so the emperor ordered that any crossbowmen taken prisoner should have their fingers cut off!

Turkish crossbowmen were also a formidable enemy. The picture on the left shows them preparing for battle outside the walls of Rhodes, in Greece, in AD 1480. In France, the development of smaller, lighter crossbows led to mounted crossbowmen carrying out cavalry attacks, shooting at the enemy as they charged in order to create panic before the main battle began. After AD 1550 the crossbow was slowly replaced on the battlefield by guns. But even after this it was used for hunting, or as a silent assassination weapon.

Turkish Soldiers, AD 1480

Fact File
European Crossbow
ca. AD 1600
Weight: 3.5 lbs. (1.6 kg)
Length: 36 in. (91.4 cm)
Range: 1,201 ft. (366 m)
In use:
ca. AD 1600–1700
Origin: Europe

QUARREL *Windlass crossbows shot deadly, four-sided bolts called quarrels (above). The word "quarrel" comes from the French word carré, meaning "square." Quarrels were usually short and heavy and were fired with such force that they could penetrate armor.*

Machines of War

Not all weapons were handheld. The most powerful weapons were too large to be operated, or even moved, by one man. These were the great engines of war that hurled rocks, fired huge bolts, and even threw dead bodies over castle walls.

Siege Engines

Some machines of war were used against troops, while others broke down the walls and doors of castles. Machines such as the battering ram and the siege tower were used to attack and break into fortified buildings.

CHARIOTS OF WAR *War chariots were first used in battle during the Bronze Age and became a key means of attack for centuries. It is said that the ancient Britons put sharp blades on the wheels of their chariots that sliced through the enemy as they charged. In ancient Egypt, the Battle of Kadesh (shown above) in 1275 BC was possibly the largest chariot battle ever fought, with almost 6,000 chariots clashing on the battlefield!*

Medieval Ballista

A Giant Crossbow

In the 400s BC, the Chinese developed a massive crossbow. A form of this weapon, known as a ballista (above), reached Europe around 350 BC. These weapons were very powerful and could shoot bolts weighing up to 11 lbs. (5 kg) over a distance of 656 ft. (200 m). The ballista was a prized weapon in the Roman army, and it was also popular in medieval Europe.

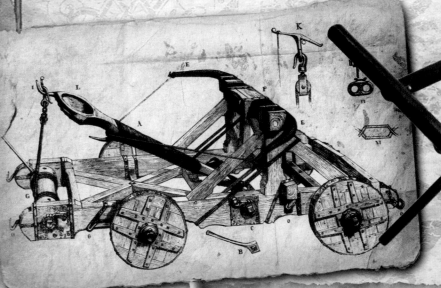

MEDIEVAL CATAPULT PLANS

Sinew Power

In the 340s BC, engineers in Macedonia invented a new way of treating animal sinew, or tendons, so that they stayed soft and springy. The Macedonians wove them together into ropes which, when twisted, exerted lots of power. They worked like giant, twisted rubber bands. They were used in a weapon called the scorpion. Two sets of sinew ropes operated a pair of levers that powered a sliding rack, which shot a bolt with tremendous force.

In about AD 250, the Romans invented a type of catapult called an onager, which means "the mule." This had a single, sinew-powered arm with a cup on the end. The arm was winched down flat and a missile, such as a large stone, was put into the cup. When it was released, the arm sprang back up, sending the missile flying through the air.

Scorpions

Small scorpions (above) could be carried in pieces on a packhorse. They were unloaded and put together in just a couple of hours. Under the rule of Alexander the Great, the Macedonians used them in several battles. Scorpions were also a favorite weapon of the Romans. If a bolt struck a group of tightly packed soldiers, it could kill several and disorder the formation.

Medieval Monsters

After the fall of the Roman Empire, only the Chinese had the skills and resources to build large war machines. But after AD 1000, rulers in Europe began building these awesome weapons again. Soon, all the ancient types of war engines were being made and used against the castles and armies of medieval Europe.

Trebuchet

The heavy weight on the end of the arm of this medieval trebuchet (left)—a type of catapult—pulled the arm up quickly, flinging the missile held in the sling at the other end towards the enemy.

Fact file
Medieval Ballista
Weight: 331 lbs. (150 kg)
Length: 16 ft. (5 m)
Range: 1,500 ft. (457 m)
In use: AD 400–1350
Origin: Europe

Deadly Ammunition *Catapults (see plans on the left) were used mainly to throw stones, but more unusual missiles were also fired. During one battle around 185 BC, Hannibal of Carthage shot small clay pots containing poisonous snakes. In AD 1346, Mongol soldiers fired the bodies of men who had died of plague, hoping to spread the disease to the enemy. And in AD 1422, the Czechs ran out of ammunition, so they hurled horse dung at the enemy instead!*

Early Guns

Huo Jian Arrow Launchers

These handheld devices were invented in China toward the end of the tenth century. They used gunpowder to launch clusters of arrows from bamboo or wooden holders.

The invention of gunpowder and the development of guns and cannons revolutionized warfare. It took fewer men to inflict more damage. Guns could be fired from a relatively safe distance, so it was less necessary for men to meet in dangerous and bloody hand-to-hand combat. As armies began to favor guns over more traditional weapons, battlefields everywhere were filled with the thundering roar of cannons and the crack of muskets.

Amazing New Inventions

Gunpowder was discovered around AD 850 by Chinese monks searching for the secret of immortality, or everlasting life. The Chinese were soon using their discovery to make new weapons such as bombs, mines, and rockets, and by the tenth century they had invented the first gun, called a fire lance.

Early guns had vase-shaped barrels and fired bolts, or arrows, rather than bullets. When they were fired, flames and smoke poured out of the barrel as the bolt flew out.

News of this incredible new invention soon spread to Europe, and by AD 1325, gunsmiths in Italy had produced a Chinese-style weapon.

Fact File
Wheel Lock Pistol
Weight: 2.5 lbs. (1.1 kg)
Length: 25–26 in. (63.5–66 cm)
Range: Up to 50 ft. (15.2 m)
In use: AD 1500–1650
Origin: Europe

European Guns

By the AD 1330s, Europeans had discovered how to make gunpowder explode more violently. This meant that guns could now be used to shoot heavy stones or lead balls instead of bolts.

In the AD 1400s, gunsmiths began producing smaller weapons for one person to use. They had long barrels into which the gunpowder and a ball were pushed. The gunpowder was set off by pushing a red-hot wire though a hole at the back of the gun. A bronze hook on the barrel was used to brace the weapon for firing against a wall or shield (above).

Early Medieval Gun

The Changing Face of Warfare

From AD 1450, guns were more accurate and could fire balls much farther. The barrels were longer and the gunpowder was lit with a smoldering piece of string called a slow match, which the soldier kept lit and ready all the time.

By AD 1476, advances in gun design resulted in a type of weapon that would be used by soldiers for the next 350 years. The barrel was about 3 ft. (1 m) long and was mounted on a wooden stock, or handle. The gun was braced against the shoulder while the soldier aimed by looking along the barrel.

German Wheel Lock Pistol, ca. AD 1640

The way that guns fired also changed. By AD 1476, the slow match was mounted on a metal lever attached to a trigger; these guns were called matchlocks (right). In the sixteenth century, guns were fired using a wheel-lock mechanism, and by the AD 1630s, the flintlock was in use. Both of these used sparks to ignite the gunpowder. The way these mechanisms worked is explained on the the far right.

Load, Aim, Fire!

To load these early guns, gunpowder was poured into the open end of the barrel, followed by the lead ball wrapped in paper or cloth to make it fit snugly. A ramrod —a metal or wooden stick—was used to push them both down. When the trigger was pulled, the gunpowder was ignited and it blasted the lead ball out of the barrel.

Matchlock Guns Being Fired

LEAD BALLS *Early guns sometimes fired stone balls, but as firearms became more advanced, they fired lead shot. Each soldier made his own lead shot before the battle by melting lead over a fire and pouring the molten lead into a special mold.*

How Firing Mechanisms Work

Matchlock, AD 1450s–1720s

When the trigger was pulled, the metal arm holding the lit slow match flicked down and into a small pan of gunpowder. The flash from this went through a small hole in the barrel and ignited the main charge inside the gun.

Wheel Lock, AD 1500–1650s

The metal grip, or cock, held a piece of iron pyrite. When the trigger was pulled, the iron pyrite fell against the grooved edge of a spinning metal wheel (which was wound up by a key). This showered sparks into the pan, igniting the main charge in the gun.

Flintlock, AD 1620s–1830s

The flintlock worked the same way as the wheel lock, by using sparks to ignite the powder in the pan. Instead of iron pyrite, however, the cock held a flint that fell against a piece of grooved metal. It became the most popular type of gun because it was better than a matchlock and cheaper than a wheel lock.

Time Line

This time line shows key events in the history of weapons and warfare. The letters BC mean that the event happened before people believe Christ was born, and the letters AD mean it happened after Christ's birth. The BC dates run backward (500 BC is longer ago than 350 BC), and the AD dates run forward: AD 75 is more recent than AD 25. Many of the dates given here are approximate. "Ca." stands for "circa," which means "about" in Latin and is used where an exact date is unknown.

ca. 1,900,000 BC
First known weapons are sharpened stone pebbles.

ca. 1,000,000 BC
The hand ax is developed.

ca. 120,000 BC
The first spears, javelins, axes, and slings are created.

ca. 40,000 BC
Bows and arrows developed.

ca. 30,000 BC
Spear-thrower invented.

ca. 4400 BC
Horses are domesticated by humans.

ca. 3500 BC
Copper is used to make axes for the first time.

ca. 800 BC
The composite bow is developed.

ca. 700 BC
Dory spears are used by the Hoplites in a phalanx formation.

Specialized javelin-throwing units appear in the Greek army.

490 BC
The Battle of Marathon, where the Greeks use thrusting spears to defeat Persians armed with javelins and swords.

480 BC
Leonidas, king of the Spartans, is killed at the Battle of Thermopylae.

ca. 350 BC
Macedonians develop the sarissa, a type of spear.

341 BC
First reliable recorded use of the crossbow by the Chinese at the Battle of Maling.

331 BC
The Battle of Gaugamela, where Macedonian king Alexander the Great conquers the vast Persian Empire.

ca. 100 BC
Gladiators in Rome start using standardized dueling weapons.

44 BC
Julius Caesar, Emperor of Rome, is assassinated.

AD 43
The Romans invade and conquer Britain using short swords against the Celts' slashing swords.

ca. AD 250
Romans invent the onager.

ca. AD 350
Romans introduce the spatha slashing sword.

ca. AD 400
Germanic peoples dominate Europe using spears and swords.

ca. AD 500
Development of the first longbows.

ca. AD 800
Double-handed Danish ax is used by Viking warriors.

AD 814
Charlemagne, ruler of the Frankish empire, dies.

AD 1095
The first Crusade to the Holy Land begins.

AD 1132
The first documented battlefield use of gunpowder cannons takes place in China.

AD 1163
Work starts on the Notre Dame Cathedral in Paris, France.

AD 1191
The Battle of Arsuf in the Holy Land, where a heavily armored and mounted army of Crusader knights, led by Richard the Lionheart of England, defeats Saladin's Muslim army.

AD 1221
The Battle of Merv, where the Mongol army of mounted men with composite bows and short swords defeats a much larger Persian army armed with lances and slashing swords. The population of Merv—about 200,000 people—was then massacred by the Mongols.

AD 1346
The Battle of Crécy, where English longbow archers (using deadly arrow-storm tactics) and dismounted, sword-wielding knights slaughter the French army.

AD 1347
The Black Death reaches Europe as it sweeps across the world.

ca. AD 1350
Knights start to use special jousting weapons during tournaments.

ca. AD 1370
The windlass crossbow is invented.

AD 1431
Joan of Arc, heroine of France, is burned at the stake.

ca. AD 1440
Matchlock gun invented.

ca. AD 1450
Infantry, or foot soldiers, start to use the pike in battle.

AD 1492
Christopher Columbus reaches America.

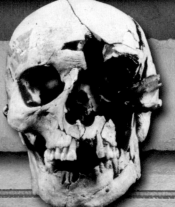

ca. 3300 BC
Spears and axes are created using bronze.

ca. 2500 BC
First stabbing swords and daggers, made from bronze, appear.

ca. 2560 BC
In Egypt, the Great Pyramids of Giza are completed.

ca. 1500 BC
The first slashing sword, a bronze "leaf" weapon, appears. Iron is produced for the first time.

1274 BC
The Battle of Kadesh, between Egyptians and Hittites, sees the first use of iron weapons in a major battle.

ca. 1000 BC
Mongolians invent the earliest known crossbows.

323 BC
Alexander the Great, king of the Macedons, dies.

216 BC
The Battle of Cannae, where Hannibal, the great Carthaginian commander, wipes out a Roman army of 80,000 men in the bloodiest day of war ever. The Carthaginians were armed with short swords and javelins, the Romans with thrusting spears.

221 BC
Work starts on the Great Wall of China.

ca. 150 BC
Romans invent the *pilum*, a specialized form of javelin.

ca. 140 BC
The soldiers of the Roman Empire adopt the *gladius* stabbing sword.

ca. AD 850
Gunpowder invented in China.

ca. AD 900
The lance is developed for use by armored horsemen.

ca. AD 950s
The first gun—a fire lance that ignites gunpowder to fire a shot, shrapnel, or arrows towards a target—is invented.

AD 1066
The Battle of Hastings, where mounted knights from Normandy equipped with lances defeat English soldiers armed with spears and swords.

AD 1070s
Work starts on the Tower of London in England.

AD 1227
Genghis Khan, ruler of the Mongols, dies.

AD 1305
William Wallace, Scottish leader, is executed.

AD 1332
The Battle of the Golden Spurs, where Flemish foot soldiers armed with simple pole weapons defeat an army of French knights.

AD 1333
The Battle of Halidon Hill, where the English first use the longbow in an arrow-storm tactic.

ca. AD 1515
Development of the first wheel lock guns.

AD 1525
The Battle of Pavia, where a Spanish-Italian army made up of infantry armed with muskets and pikes defeats the French-Swiss cavalry.

ca. AD 1550s
Invention of the rapier sword.

AD 1564
William Shakespeare, English playwright, is born.

ca. AD 1610
Development of the first flintlock gun.

AD 1760s
Pairs of pistols are introduced for dueling.

Picture Credits

The publishers would like to thank the following sources for their kind permission to reproduce the pictures in this book. Every effort has been made to acknowledge correctly and contact the source and/or copyright-holder of each picture and Carlton Books Limited apologizes for any unintentional errors or omissions, which will be corrected in future editions of this book.

Photograph indicators: t-top, b-bottom, l-left, c-centre, r-right.
Pages are numbered as follows: Title endpaper 2/3; Stone to Metal 4/5; Spears 6/7; Javelins 8/9; Short Swords 10/11; Long Swords 12/13; Maces 14/15; Axes 16/17; Pole Arms 18/19; Dueling Weapons 20/21; Bows 22/23; Crossbows 24/25; Machines of War 26/27; Early Guns 28/29; Time Line endpaper 30/31.

AKG-Images: /Erich Lessing: 7l, 10c, 21bl. Alamy: /Stefano Arcidiacono: 15c; /Alastair Balderstone: 23bl; /BlueMoon Stock: 19br; /Jake Corke: 23tc; /Interfoto Pressebildagentur: 14tr. Arms & Armor Inc.: 19tr. BARC, Archaeological Sciences, University of Bradford: 12bl, 19r, 30br. George Barrow: 7bl. The Bridgeman Art Library: /James Gillray/© Courtesy of the Warden and Scholars of New College, Oxford: 9br; /© Look and Learn: 23bc; /Museum of London: 10bl. Carlton Books: /Russell Porter: 3, 9l, 12r, 17tr, 19tl, 21t, 23tr, 27tr, 27bl, 30bl, 31b. Corbis: /The Art Archive: 22tl; /Christel Gerstenberg: 26, 32-catapult plans; /Bettmann: 9tr, 25tr; /Stefano Bianchetti: 5tl; /Historical Picture Archive: 13c; /Charles & Josette Lenars: 5b; /James W. Porter: 4tl; /Stapleton Collection: 18bl, 26tl; /Werner Forman: 17tl. Dorling Kindersley: 5tr, 6tl, 7tr, 8tl, 8-9, 15b, 26-27; /Geoff Brightling/Courtesy of the Order of the Black Prince: 28br; 18-Swiss Halbeard pole arms; /Andy Crawford: 10tr, 12bc; /Geoff Dann: 22r, 24br; /Geoff Dann/The Wallace Collection: 14c, 28c, 29r; /Peter Dennis: 6br; /Eddie Gerald: 24l; /Dave King: 10-11, 12c; /James Stevenson: 28tl; /Geoff Brightling: 18br. Peter Engerisser: 29c, 29tr. Getty Images: /Karl Bodmer/The Bridgeman Art Library: 16bl; /The Bridgeman Art Library: 25l; /Steve Cole/Photodisc: 4bl; /Ernst Haas: 22bl; /John Heaviside Clark/The Bridgeman Art Library: 8c; /Vincent Clarence Scott O'Connor/The Bridgeman Art Library: 5r; /Heinrich Van Den Berg/Gallo Images: 7br. Xavier Gille: 21br. Imagestate: /The Board of Trustees of the Armories/Heritage-Images: 11br, 17br, 20r, 27bc, /British Library/Heritage-Images: 17bl; /Herve Champollion/TOP: 4c; /CM Dixon/Heritage-Images: 6tr; /Museum of London/Heritage-Images: 4-5; /The Print Collector/Heritage-Images: 20l. iStockphoto.com: 4br, 22br. Greg Kowal: 16r, 30-31c. Mary Evans Picture Library: 9tl, 12tl. National Maritime Museum: 29br. PA Photos: /David Cheskin: 17tc. The Picture Desk: /Gianni Dagli Orti/Musee Conde Chantilly/The Art Archive: 11r; /Gianni Dagli Orti/Museo Etnografico Pigorini Rome/The Art Archive: 8bl; /Gianni Dagli Orti/Musee Archeologique Naples/The Art Archive: 6bl. Private Collection: 19bl. Rex Features: /© 20th Century Fox/Everett Collection: 13tl; /SNAP: 23br; /© Warner Brothers/Everett Collection: 10tl. Royal Armories Image Library: 5tc, 13bl, 13tr, 15l, 16l, 18c, 20br, 24-25, 25b. Topfoto.co.uk: /Print Collector/HIP: 14bl. Chris Vinten: 13r. Wikipedia: 15tr.